Effective
Communication Skills

Dalton Kehoe, Ph.D.

THE
GREAT
COURSES®

PUBLISHED BY:

THE GREAT COURSES
Corporate Headquarters
4840 Westfields Boulevard, Suite 500
Chantilly, Virginia 20151-2299
Phone: 1-800-832-2412
Fax: 703-378-3819
www.thegreatcourses.com

Dalton Kehoe, Ph.D.

Senior Scholar of Communications
York University

Professor Dalton Kehoe has been a teacher and organizational change practitioner for more than 41 years. Recently retired as Associate Professor from York University in Toronto, Ontario, he is now Senior Scholar of Communications in the university's Communication Studies Department. He specializes in interpersonal and organizational communications and continues to administer two online courses on these subjects for his department. He received a B.A. in Business Administration from the University of Toledo in 1964, an M.A. in Sociology from the University of Cincinnati in 1967, and a Ph.D. in Social Psychology from York University in 1973.

Professor Kehoe is also senior partner of Heart of the Matter Consulting, a firm dedicated to helping organizations reengage their employees. As a public speaker, he presents seminars to organizations in the United States and Canada on the use of technology in teaching and on leadership and employee engagement.

His research interests involve two areas: grant-funded investigations of the effects of using video-streaming technology in blended-learning classes (live tutorials plus online lecturing), and the effects of leadership communication on employees' engagement in their work.

Professor Kehoe's recent publications include *Communication in Everyday Life* (2nd ed.) and *Communicating in Organizations: Complexity, Constraint and Creative Choice* (both published by Pearson Education Canada).

Professor Kehoe was the first academic in North America to use Mediasite Live streaming technology in his classes as part of their blended-learning format. His research on student responses to video streaming led to significant changes in the way he taught online. His work has been recognized at the national level by *The Chronicle of Higher Education* in the United States and by *University Affairs* in Canada.

Early in his career, Professor Kehoe was recognized by his colleagues as one of the top 10 teachers in Ontario. In 1997 he won a York University teaching award, and in 2006 he was recognized as one of the top 30 professors in Ontario by the province's public educational network, TVO. Professor Kehoe was also one of the highest-rated workshop leaders for the Executive Education Center of York's Schulich School of Business. ■

Table of Contents

INTRODUCTION

Professor Biography i
Course Scope 1

LECTURE GUIDES

LECTURE 1
The Magic of Everyday Communication 3

LECTURE 2
The Complex Layers of Face-to-Face Talk 6

LECTURE 3
The Social Context That Shapes Our Talk 9

LECTURE 4
The Operations of the Cognitive Unconscious 12

LECTURE 5
The Conscious Mind in Perception 15

LECTURE 6
The Conscious Mind in Using Language 18

LECTURE 7
The Conscious Mind and Emotion 21

LECTURE 8
The Development of Our Sense of Self 24

LECTURE 9
Self, Attachment, and Self-Esteem 28

LECTURE 10
Protecting the Self in Face-to-Face Talk 32

Table of Contents

LECTURE 11
Conscious Self-Talk and Self-Management......................................35

LECTURE 12
Challenges to Effective Communication 38

LECTURE 13
Talking to Connect and Build Relationships 40

LECTURE 14
Differences, Disagreement, and Control Talk 43

LECTURE 15
Commands, Accusations, and Blame 46

LECTURE 16
Healing Relationships with Dialogue Talk...49

LECTURE 17
Focus on the Other—The Heart of Dialogue 52

LECTURE 18
Assertive Dialogue to Manage Disagreement 55

LECTURE 19
Compassionate Confrontation 58

LECTURE 20
Communication, Gender, and Culture 61

LECTURE 21
Talking Our Way to Lasting Relationships 64

LECTURE 22
Leadership, Appreciation, and Productivity 67

Table of Contents

LECTURE 23
Dialogue and Appreciation—Engaged Employees 70

LECTURE 24
Dialogue—Ethical Choices behind Our Talk 73

SUPPLEMENTAL MATERIAL

Bibliography..76

Effective Communication Skills

Scope:

Asa humans, we need to sustain relationships with others in order to get what we think we need and want from life. To do this, we use a collection of behaviors described as communication skills. Although we use them every day in our lives, we are often unaware of how they develop and function. This course provides a theoretical and practical survey of the ideas behind, and the practices of, effective communication.

Our first goal is awareness. We begin to become aware of how face-to-face talk really works by comparing our commonsense views of talk with the fundamental models developed by communication researchers and theorists over the past 60 years. We investigate the essential processes that permit us to communicate—to understand and be understood by others—and discover that many of these processes are so deeply learned that they operate automatically in most situations.

The next step in our journey to awareness is to reveal the automatic and hidden processes that influence everyday talk, including our deep cultural learning and the nonconscious part of the mind, where much of this learning is stored. We then discuss how they affect our conscious mind while we're in conversation with ourselves or another person. It turns out that seeing what's real and right in front of us—and responding accordingly—is not as easy as we think. Moreover, these processes don't operate independently of each other; they work through our sense of self. Instead of seeing the world the way it is, we see it the way we are. This course explores how our unique and conscious sense of self develops and how we evaluate and defend it, while it shapes how we see, think, and feel about others. At the end of each lecture, exercises are provided to help you become more conscious of these forces in your talk and to help you deal with them to become a better communicator.

The second goal of this course is effective action in our daily talk. We take an overview of the ideals of effective talk and learn to divide face-to-face talk into three easily recognized modes: connect talk, which describes the essential exchanges we make every day to create and sustain relationships; control talk, which is our automatic response to dealing with differences, disagreements, or disorder in our relationships; and dialogue talk, which is the talk of conscious choice and self-management. You will learn exactly when, where, and how to use the elements of dialogue talk so that you and the other person can create a workable connection even in complicated and emotionally fraught situations.

Later lectures analyze three vital contexts where positive, clear, and enabling communication is critical—the continuing conversation between the genders, and between people trying to build and sustain positive relationships in their personal lives and in the workplace. We end our course with a lecture intended to remind us that everyday talk is an arena of constant struggle between quick, automatic, judgmental reactions that distance us from the reality of the moment and slower responses based on conscious awareness and acceptance of what's facing us here and now. Every time we are in a difficult conversation with someone and we make a conscious choice to slow our emotional reactions and speak in ways that enable both of us to move toward mutual understanding, we add goodness to life. Effective talk is more than simply practical; it is fundamentally ethical. ■

The Magic of Everyday Communication
Lecture 1

Our cultural learning tells us that talk is about influential talk—saying the right words in the right way. We often think of conversation as a contest if someone disagrees with us. Our minds are wired to think of ourselves as better-than-average in everyday situations, and when our thoughts are challenged, we naturally think of ourselves as right. All of these tendencies compel in us a view that talk is fundamentally simple and that if someone doesn't understand us, it must be their fault. But there is a great deal more to our talk than our surface assumptions suggest—to become better, we need to know more and blame less.

In these lectures, I hope to take talk out of the realm of the automatic and make us all aware of what gets in the way of being effective communicators. Getting better at this vital skill is challenging but not impossible. We will focus not only on how we perform the magic act of speaking but also, and perhaps more importantly, on those situations where the magic doesn't seem to work.

Effectiveness in communication means three things: First, we got what we wanted—a moment of positive emotional connection or a tangible result. Second, we've been understood from our point of view (and that was communicated back to us). And third, the other party seems fine with the exchange—there were no indications of uncertainty, frustration, fear, or anger.

You don't generally notice all of the background structuring that makes your talk understood. You have a picture in your mind of a particular reality that you want to communicate. To speak, you have to quickly pull together a collection of words whose single, clear meaning will describe your image, and you have to assemble them into a recognizably ordered, nongraphical message. You then utter the sound elements representing these verbal symbols in a way that you assume the other will recognize; along with these utterances, you also transmit a set of nonverbal gestures (hand gestures, facial movement, and voice intonation). You send all of this to the ears and eyes of another person in certain belief that that person will hear and see everything you said and stay mentally focused for the entire message. The listener must then decode your message correctly, picking your meanings (not theirs) from the archive of meanings they have accumulated based on their previous experience (not yours). The listener must also avoid misinterpreting any of your words because of unintended and unconscious nonverbals and then translate this verbal message into the same picture in her mind as you have in yours, without any distracting internal thoughts, feelings, or beliefs of her own.

Successful communication is a much more complicated process than we tend to realize.

Communication experts are aware of how humorously disconnected the common view of communication can be from the complex reality. Here are the amusing communication "laws" written by Osmo A. Wiio, a Finnish professor of communication: (1) Communication usually fails, except by accident. (2) If a message can be interpreted in several ways, it will be interpreted in a manner that maximizes damage. (3) There is always someone who knows better than you what you meant by your message. Think of these as Murphy's laws of talk: If anything can go wrong, it will. Rest assured that throughout this course, I will point out such pitfalls and give you ways to overcome them. ∎

1. Think of a situation where you talked directly with another about something you wanted or needed, but you didn't get it. As you recall the scene, notice the first emotional reaction you remember having. Was it positive or negative? Did you call up a label for the other person or the way he or she talked to you? We will look at these natural reactions as we move through the first section of the course.

2. Is there a situation in the recent past where looking back, you feel the other person didn't really listen to you and what you had to say, and had the person listened to you, the outcome would have been better—for you and for the other person? How do you feel about this situation now when you recall it? Remember this feeling—we will return to the importance of listening later in the course.

The Complex Layers of Face-to-Face Talk
Lecture 2

Interpersonal communication is a process whereby two or more people within a particular context and who are aware of each other act together to create and manage shared meetings. All of this goes on through nonconscious display or conscious sending and receiving of messages using a shared repertoire of both verbal and nonverbal symbols.

The model of face-to-face communication developed by communication theorists and researchers over the past 50 years reveals what is actually happening as we talk with one another. It turns out that what we say between the lines about ourselves and our relationship to the other actually shapes the meaning of the lines we deliver about the conversational topic. This is an important revelation because it helps to explain why we are effective communicators in some situations and not in others.

By the 1950s, we had put together a basic model that says every face-to-face moment has a sender, a message, channels, and a receiver. We also added two additional concepts: noise (anything that interferes with the sending of a message) and feedback (the receiver's immediate verbal response to whatever the sender said). As the model began to work, scientists came to recognize that what's in people's heads actually isn't noise but rather their personal experience. What the receiver got from our words may not be our meanings but the meanings they put into the words as they were coming in.

What's interesting about this is it shifts our focus from the sender to the receiver. After 2,000 years of rhetorical analysis focused on the sender, we put the receiver—the other—at the center of our analysis. As our thinking and research progressed, we also realized we needed to move away from our traditional emphasis on words to a focus on the relationship between words and nonverbal displays in our analysis of the continuous and simultaneous flow of messages.

The system of face-to-face talk is outlined in a set of axioms that were published by Paul Watzlawick in one of the classic treatises on interpersonal talk, *Pragmatics of Human Communication*. The first axiom is that in face-to-face situations, communication is inevitable. You don't have to say a word; as soon as you're in somebody's sight, you're telling them something. The second axiom says that face-to-face communication always combines words and nonverbals. What you say and how you say it is tied together—and these two levels can reinforce or contradict each other. The third axiom is that it's always about content and relationship at the same time. The fourth axiom says that all communication is either symmetrical or complementary. Face-to-face communication is a process of mutual exchange and adjustment, and the fifth axiom is that this process is punctuated differently by each of the participants.

Face-to-face communication is a process of mutual exchange and adjustment.

Our model includes external communication and internal feedback as well as messages working at two levels (topic and relationship feedback) that happen instantaneously, also at two levels (verbal and nonverbal). People are senders and receivers at the same time—encoding and decoding while talking to themselves very, very quickly, all while talking to somebody else. If it seems very complicated, it is! But rather than focus on the complexity, look at what this model does. It gives us many more ways of understanding how talk works; perhaps more importantly, it gives us explanations for why talk doesn't always work. ■

Suggested Reading

Barnlund, "Towards a Meaning-Centered Philosophy."

Devito, *The Interpersonal Communication Book.*

Stewart, *Bridges Not Walls.*

Watzlawick, Bavelas, and Jackson, *Pragmatics of Human Communication.*

1. Think of a time when you were talking to someone—when you thought you were being perfectly clear, but they didn't seem to get it. How might the concept of noise help you explain why this moment of ineffective communication happened?

2. Listen carefully as someone tells you about a conversation with somebody else that didn't go well (or remember someone telling you such a story recently). As you listen or remember, recall the fifth fundamental axiom of the interpersonal communication model: People punctuate the flow of talk to serve themselves. Does this help to explain the way the story unfolds?

The Social Context That Shapes Our Talk
Lecture 3

In the previous lecture, we talked about the context that surrounds our moment of talk and shapes the meanings of our words and gestures. Now we discuss the biggest context of all: our society's culture. In our everyday talk, our cultural learning automatically provides us two things: a perspective on life and a storehouse of knowledge about the physical and social worlds we inhabit.

Culture is the way of life that one generation teaches to the next so the new generation can see the world the "right" way and behave as "normal" members of the group. We call this form of teaching socialization. Every society communicates such standards of achievement and appropriate behavior. For life in general they are called values, and for situations they are called norms.

It is interesting that at the societal level, one of the ways we have come to understand our key values and our ways of talking has been to compare our society to others. Let's look at two of the dimensions along which cultures can be compared. The first dimension has to do with values. The United States is an individualist culture, like Britain and many European countries: We tend to focus on how events affect individuals or how individual actions change other individuals. We place a greater emphasis on personal accomplishments and on standing out from the crowd. Many Asian societies are collectivist cultures: Talk there focuses more on family and community—and individual responsibility to them. Success is measured by a person's contribution to the achievements of the group as a whole, and people tend to take pride in their similarity to other members of their group.

The second dimension has to do with the norms of appropriate manner. Cultures require different degrees of physical or psychological closeness between people for them to be effective as communicators. In high expressive cultures (such as South America and southern Europe), talkers immediately communicate warmth, closeness, and availability, including through physical contact. In low expressive cultures (including North America and northern

Europe), people tend to talk first and maybe shake a hand at the end.

The essential categories of shared meaning are words and nonverbals. Words are essential but slippery tools; they simply refer to or stand for something else, so we have to agree on and memorize their meanings. Words may also carry personal

Cultures differ in the amount of emphasis they place on the individual versus the group.

meanings (connotations) for you and members of your group that are not widely shared. The multiplicity of denotative meanings plus the possibility of uniqueness of connotative meanings are reasons for a good deal of the uncertainty in our talk.

Beyond words, we use the meanings of facial and body gestures. In situations where we're not sure what people are saying, we lean heavily on how they look and sound. The impact of a message on the receiver is based not on what was said but how it was said. Nonverbals seem to operate in three ways in our face-to-face communication: They affect the meanings conveyed verbally, they shape the type of relationship that we are creating with another person, and they directly communicate our emotions before and during talk. ■

Suggested Reading

Aronson, Wilson, et al., *Social Psychology.*

Cohen and Nisbett, *Culture of Honor.*

Ekman, *Emotions Revealed.*

Finegan, *Language.*

Gladwell, *Outliers.*

Hofstede, *Culture's Consequences.*

Jandt, *An Introduction to Intercultural Communication.*

Leathers, *Successful Nonverbal Communication.*

Mehrabian, *Nonverbal Communication.*

Tannen, *You Just Don't Understand.*

Exercises

1. The next time you are confronted by someone with a very different speaking style (more warmly intense or coolly distant than yours) or whose talk seems to emphasize different values than yours, instead of saying, "What's wrong with this person?" you could ask yourself, "I wonder where this person comes from?" This gives you more to work with in understanding others.

2. Can you think of a time when someone spoke to you (or you saw someone speaking) where you felt that the person's words and gestures didn't match? What was your first reaction to the mismatch? Did you believe the person?

The Operations of the Cognitive Unconscious
Lecture 4

The cognitive unconscious is a part of our mind to which our conscious mind has no direct access because its memories are not constructed of words and pictures but biochemical patterns. These patterns give shape to every word we say. This lecture explores three aspects of the cognitive unconscious: the operations of the cognitive unconscious (how it gets us through our day), the three areas of decision making by the cognitive unconscious that permit us to speak and act normally, and the effects (both positive and negative) of these unconscious decisions on our communication relationships.

The cognitive unconscious works in a completely different way than the conscious mind: It's automatic, fast, and rigid. It just sees and acts; there is no creative reflection in the cognitive unconscious—just pattern detection. Unlike your conscious brain, it's always paying attention. Every waking second as we grow, the cognitive unconscious is processing incoming data, looking for patterns in the information that flows from the rest of our bodies or from the environment around us. It remembers these patterns by giving them emotional markers. The cognitive unconscious organizes and stores our deeply learned patterns of perception and preference for people and actions.

There are three key functions that the cognitive unconscious carries out on behalf of the conscious mind. (1) It supports rational decision making. Since the time of Aristotle, we had believed that the conscious did all the work of deciding, but we now know that without the support of the cognitive unconscious, we simply couldn't make decisions at all. (2) The cognitive unconscious constantly evaluates the world around us. It senses what's going on before our conscious mind does, and its first impressions can be extremely accurate most of the time. (3) It initiates action in a sophisticated and efficient manner. The cognitive unconscious knows what's going to happen next, and the limbic system is far faster than the conscious mind at making decisions.

Let's look at the impacts of these types of unconscious decisions on our communication in relationships. We simply couldn't talk effectively without the speed and automaticity that the cognitive unconscious gives us; it allows us to automatically invoke the normal conversation schema we discussed in Lecture 3. We can uncover word meanings with little hesitation and read the meaning of others' nonverbal displays as the words are being spoken. But the cognitive unconscious isn't perfect, and when it goes wrong,

From the time we are born, our cognitive unconscious is gathering data and looking for patterns to help us communicate.

it can go very wrong. If the external situation changes rapidly from positive to negative, the part of the mind that presents us our ideas to smoothly read situations so we can speak with confidence can suddenly turn against us.

Unlike first responder professionals, we are not deeply trained to handle difficult situations before they happen. This is, in fact, the entire reason for our course—to become like first responder professionals in our communication emergencies. By the time you finish this course, you will have tools to do this. ■

Suggested Reading

Aronson, Wilson, et al., *Social Psychology.*

Fine, *A Mind of Its Own.*

Gladwell, *Blink.*

Pentland, *Honest Signals.*

Restak, *The Naked Brain.*

Wilson, *Strangers to Ourselves.*

1. Remember a time when someone made a great first impression on you. You really liked him or her the moment you met; you talked easily to each other, as if you'd known each other for years. Try to reconstruct what it was that attracted you to the person.

2. Think about the last time you really lost your temper or witnessed someone else lose theirs. Did you (or the other person) demonstrate the key elements of this overwhelming moment that we discussed in the lecture? If it was you who "lost it," how did the event leave you feeling when it was over?

The Conscious Mind in Perception
Lecture 5

To understand why we talk the way we do and in order to talk more effectively, we need to analyze three interrelated processes at work in the conscious mind: how we see things, how we think about things, and how we feel about things. The first of these refers to the process of perception: selecting, organizing, and interpreting incoming data. This lecture explores how these processes work to organize our images of the world around us, ourselves and our behavior, and other people and how they behave.

When something gets our conscious attention, the conscious mind uses a three-step process. It selects what to see, it organizes that data into patterns, and it interprets the pattern (gives it meaning by a quick compare-contrast with the patterns we have already learned). In most of the moments in our daily lives, we tend to be low-effort decision makers, using schemas for perceptual processing. When we are perceiving the world around us, consistency is key. We consciously work to achieve consistency between our perceptions of self, our own behavior, and feedback from the world around us.

Remember that the selective attention process chooses what to look at based on intensity and novelty and then organizes what it has selected into patterns. If the world doesn't respond to us or our behavior in ways that we find consistent with our perceptions of ourselves, and if we can't change the incoming data, we tend to ignore or distort it—this is an automatic response. So, for example, if you believe you are a capable, kindly, and attentive spouse, and your mate criticizes you for being incompetent, cruel, and dismissive, you might either attribute the message to your mate having had a bad day at work or to his or her playing a strange joke on you.

This process is supported by the unconscious operations of the mind as well; it's hard to change a mind. But there is a way to change your perceptions of yourself and your behavior. We can change our perceptions if we choose to be consciously involved in learning. We have to be willing to go outside our comfort zone and do hard, often painful, conscious work.

We've been dealing with the perceptions of one's self and behavior; what about how we see other people? People are complex, and seeing them should be more complex than seeing things. But our perceptions of people are simple, internally and externally consistent, and stable across time—just like the way we see ourselves, our behavior, and the world around us. Unless the situation compels us to do otherwise, we work quickly. We tend to have first impressions of people as a coherent, unified whole. We organize our perceptions around key dimensions, such as cold versus warm, and dominant versus supportive. The culture provides schematic, prepackaged realities for interpreting people and their actions. We tend to generalize about individuals based on their membership in a group. This is a shortcut to communication— but not to understanding. ■

> **In most of the moments in our daily lives, we tend to be low-effort decision makers, using schemas for perceptual processing.**

Suggested Reading

Hallinan, *Why We Make Mistakes.*

Tavris and Aronson, "Mistakes Were Made."

Exercises

1. Accept that you (like everyone) have perceptual biases, or at least that you may have them. Sometimes it helps to talk about this with a family member who may also have internalized some of the same schema or stereotypes. Sometimes it helps to ask a friend if he or she has noticed you reacting to what you think is going on rather than what actually is. (Note: Have this conversation when you are feeling particularly calm and open to listening without defense. Ask a kind friend who will be honest but gentle.)

2. Practice overriding your unconscious mind's quick, automatic response to organizing everything—slow down deliberately, and challenge yourself to see the situation differently. Get conscious.

3. If things happen that you don't like in a situation, don't jump to conclusions about your innocence—you are both involved somehow. Instead of an instant evaluation or judgment, try to respond with a hypothesis. Then talk with the person: Describe your perceptions, and ask for confirmation. Ask about the other's motives, and then listen to the answer. Don't tell the other what he or she thinks or feels.

The Conscious Mind in Using Language
Lecture 6

The cognition process involves how we name and think about the patterns we create and also how we deal with differences between our expectations and reality in day-to-day life. Our conscious mind can and does work its way through the process of rational problem solving and decision making, but it's a relatively slow, energy-demanding process. Everyday talk, however, demands a quicker form of cognition—we size up a new situation very quickly, figuring out what's going on and guessing what's going to happen next using the schema from our life experience. We effortlessly create first impressions of people and things in our environment and then interact using low effort, automatic forms of thought. But the more automatic and low-effort our thinking processes, the more vulnerable we are to mistakes that can interfere with good communication.

We should be careful in our use of words, but we aren't. Thinking about our thinking is hard work, so instead we use abstract judgment words as part of our thinking process. Humans really like using abstract and judgmental language: It rewards our sense of competent self. We sound clear, definite, and sure of ourselves—and we get other people's attention with these kinds of assertions. But when we talk like this, things can go very wrong, very quickly. Poor word choices, spoken in inappropriate contexts, can get us into trouble because we can't know for sure how others will understand our judgments.

We use four simple judgment tools to make decisions about what's going on. (1) We take things at face value. What we hear first can act as a starting point for subsequent decision making (so be careful what you say first to another). (2) We base our judgments on the ease of availability: We seem to think that the easier something is to recall, the truer it must be. (3) We use the representativeness approach, classifying a person or situation based on a case in our past. (4) We treat assumptions as facts, because we have a hard time distinguishing between inferences and observable facts.

The inference ladder is a communication model that explains how the mind moves upward from many facts to a few judgments—from description to abstraction. At the wider bottom rung of the ladder, we have observable data. We are immersed in a sea of data, and our nonconscious mind manages all this through the perception process. At the next rung of the ladder we select data, add meanings to it (cultural and personal), and produce lasting patterns. We tap into these patterns to deal with reality as best we can, but our mind leaves out lots of the new bits because they don't fit the old bits. When called upon to fit one or more of these patterns into current reality, our mind simply makes stuff up. Thus the next rung of the ladder says our mind makes inferences about what the current moment is like based on what we know from the past. We do this in a rapid, automatic fashion.

We seem to think that the easier something is to recall, the truer it must be.

In most conversation, these first rungs are handled automatically by the cognitive unconscious part of the mind. At the next rung of the ladder, we consciously draw conclusions about the external situation on the basis of our invented internal reality. Not only to do we make up our conscious minds, but we also respond to the surge of emotional energy delivered by our cognitive unconscious as we reach a decision. Because we are conscious of our beliefs, at the next rung we have to massage our conclusion to fit our beliefs. Finally, at the highest rung, we talk. We think we are acting in the moment, but the reality is at the bottom of the ladder. What you act and think on is a much higher level of emotionally energized abstraction, five steps above the reality of the now. ∎

Suggested Reading

Devito, *The Interpersonal Communication Book.*

Hallinan, *Why We Make Mistakes.*

Exercises

1. Look for meaning in people, not in words—look behind the denotative meaning of the words being used. Remember the perception process: You only have schema to work with, not reality.

2. Be aware of the quality of your information—distinguish between facts and assumptions (inferences). When facing disagreement, differences, and disorder, get down the inference ladder. Make your thinking processes, and the other person's, a part of the information being exchanged. Tell each other your thought processes, and ask questions. This will help you both stay more focused on the realities being described than the feelings hidden underneath our labels and judgments.

The Conscious Mind and Emotion
Lecture 7

As information flows through our perception and cognition processes, we notice bodily changes. For instance, edgy, fidgeting body movements and tension in the shoulders and neck may give way to a moment of stillness in the body, dropping of the shoulders, and unclenching of fingers. Our muscles are responding automatically to biochemical changes; once we become aware of these physical reactions, we call them our feelings. Our individual awareness of and ability to talk about feelings varies significantly. Few people are conscious of the interaction between our feeling and thinking processes and their effect on the way we communicate with each other. In this lecture, I will describe how developing an awareness of our feelings, naming them, and describing them accurately to ourselves and others is central to our becoming more effective communicators.

There are always three levels of reaction to a changing situation: emotions, which are the biochemical response to changes; rapid bodily reactions to those biochemical shifts; and your cognitive brain, where the left frontal lobe interprets these reactions and then names them as feelings.

Feelings are our way of noticing emotions that require attention and interrupt cognitive processes and behaviors. After the immediate feeling has subsided, it usually lingers on in the form of a mood. Does mood matter? Feelings and mood matter mostly when we're not paying attention, because when we do notice our situation, mood doesn't affect our opinions. When we're not consciously thinking, we automatically let our current feeling state shape our decision making.

We have been consistently discussing face-to-face talk in personal relationships, but there is much evidence of the effects of feelings in the workplace too. Feelings and moods are contagious: In 70 work teams across diverse industries, members who sat in meetings together ended up sharing moods—good or bad—within 2 hours. Feeling good makes people more

Positive emotions at work can lead to better teamwork and greater efficiency.

mentally efficient, better at understanding information, and view others or events in a more positive light. A positive mood also makes employees more optimistic about their abilities, more creative, and predisposed to be helpful.

To be more effective communicators, we have to become more emotionally intelligent. This concept was introduced to the public in 1995 by Daniel Goleman in his book *Emotional Intelligence.* The psychologist Reuven Bar-On defined emotional intelligence as "our ability to recognize, understand and use emotions to cope with ourselves, others and the environment." There are several important recurrent findings in the research into emotional intelligence: People who can read their own emotions and recognize their impact are likely to be good at reading others' emotional states. They also seem to be more aware of their overall strengths and limitations, which contributes to a sound sense of one's self-worth and capabilities. People who can manage their feeling reactions—who can keep their disruptive emotions and impulses under control, particularly in difficult situations—are seen as more trustworthy, honest, and of high integrity. And those who are more emotionally flexible in adapting to new situations, including seeing the upside of events, are seen as more effective managers. ∎

Suggested Reading

Ekman, *Emotions Revealed.*

Plutchik, *The Psychology and Biology of Emotion.*

Exercises

1. Try to describe your feelings accurately to yourself—and think before you speak. Before launching into a thoughtless tirade about how you feel, using vague labels like "mad" or "great," try to describe how your body feels, such as "I'm shaking like a leaf," or "I feel all tied up in knots." These statements are more accurate and don't leave the other person wondering what's really going on. Remember that you can be feeling several emotions at once.

2. Identify reasons for your feelings—you and the other need to know what triggered you in this situation. Be sure to anchor in the present, speak directly, and avoid allness statements (e.g., "I'm always ..." or "You never ..."). Don't just blow off steam or collapse into tears; say what you want the listener to do.

The Development of Our Sense of Self
Lecture 8

In the past three lectures, we have reviewed the key processes of the conscious mind separately to clarify their operations, but in reality, they operate in a fully integrated way through a unique collection of perceptions, beliefs, and feelings called the self. Unlike other creatures, we think about ourselves as separate from the world. This unique sense of separateness shapes the way our mind processes external reality, so we need to understand how our sense of self emerges out of and then continues to shape our relationships with others. In this lecture, we review several facets of this, our most cherished set of perceptions, beliefs, and feelings.

There are three aspects of the self: personality, self-concept, and self-esteem. We'll look at the first two in this lecture and save self-esteem for the next. Personality is broadly defined as an enduring set of characteristics—needs, perceptions, and emotional reactions—that influence our reactions to the world across a variety of situations. There are recognizable differences between people in terms of psychological functions; the way they use their minds is partly inherited and partly shaped in early learning.

The Myers-Briggs Type Indicator helps reveal the ways our conscious mind processes information to get us through our everyday lives. The first of four dimensions is extraversion-introversion: When life presents you a question, where do you find information? Do you turn your energy inward or call out to the world around you? The argument is that extroverted folks tend to think about things while they're talking whereas folks with a preference for introversion think about things before they talk.

The Myers-Briggs questionnaire also locates people on two dimensions of internal information processing and decision making. The first is the sensing-intuitive dimension: How do you prefer to have information organized for processing? Sensors tend to look at the world in terms of facts, routines, details, and sequential approach. Intuitives tend to look at the big picture first and then seek confirming facts. They see it all at once, but they take a more random approach to collecting facts because they already have the answer in their minds. The second internal function is the thinking-feeling dimension: How do you decide about what you've received? Thinkers tend to focus on objective analysis and rational connections between elements. Feelers take things more personally, focusing on larger values and emotional reactions by them and others to a situation.

Myers and Briggs locate each individual on one more dimension: Orientation to the world. Once you've shaped the info, once you've decided about it, how do you respond to the world? Judgers are structured, scheduled, ordered, planned, decisive, and deliberate; perceivers are flexible, spontaneous, adaptive, responsive to the situation, and tend to keep collecting data.

> **We all use all eight of these personality functions but have strong, automatic preferences for one over the other on each dimension.**

We all use all eight of these personality functions but have strong, automatic preferences for one over the other on each dimension. When we understand this about ourselves and others, we can anticipate possible issues that will arise in communication relationships and learn to manage our responses to others in ways that will allow us to be understood—and allow us to understand others.

Everyone agrees that personality is slow to change throughout our lives. Our self-concept, despite our denial of this, is always in the process of changing. Self-concept is established, sustained, and altered through communication with others and is built on the foundation of our inherited temperaments and how these were responded to by our caretakers in our earliest communication relationships. Sometimes we consciously enhance or hide parts of our self-story to make our communication work. We naturally alter the outside edges of our self as we learn and try new things; this is mostly done unthinkingly. Finally, our self-concept anchors our attitudes and judgments: We never approach situations neutrally. Our self is the position from which we look at the world; we see it the way we are, not the way it is. Our self-concept is the narrative that holds our lives together—some argue that this is the primary role of the conscious mind in human life. ∎

Suggested Reading

Falikowski, *Mastering Human Relations.*

Wood, *Spinning the Symbolic Web.*

Tips for Effective Talk across Personality Types

1. **Introverts communicating with extroverts:** Publicly state your agreements and disagreements. Don't leave others to figure out what you're thinking.

2. **Extroverts communicating with introverts:** Take the time to listen, and allow introverts time to reflect before responding to you.

3. **Sensors communicating with intuitives:** Personal experience tends to make sensors overconfident in their opinions and conclusions. Don't overgeneralize; confidence is not the same as truth.

4. **Intuitives communicating with sensors:** Base your opinions and suggestions on factual information. You can gain the confidence of sensors by connecting your opinions and suggestions to hard evidence.

5. **Thinkers communicating with feelers:** Thinkers consider their rationality and objectivity to be virtues, but critical objectivity can be perceived as callous. Before attacking others' ideas, take the time to understand and appreciate what they mean.

6. **Feelers communicating with thinkers:** Get to the point. While other feelers like you may appreciate time-consuming communication, thinkers will probably not.

7. **Judgers communicating with perceivers:** Don't jump to conclusions. Judgers prefer to make quick decisions and move on, but the desire for closure can cause them to make decisions prematurely.

8. **Perceivers communicating with judgers:** Be less vague. Perceivers like to keep their options open, but their constant consideration of possibilities can represent vagueness and lack of preparation to judgers.

Self, Attachment, and Self-Esteem
Lecture 9

In this lecture, we consider how self-esteem develops and what emotions are involved in the process. We also look at how we manage our self-perceptions and our self-presentation to preserve our self-esteem in our daily interactions with others. To do this, we use a simple model of self-awareness called the Johari window.

The Johari window (see Figure 9.1) is a simple table built around two dimensions—what you do or don't consciously know about yourself and what others do or don't know about you. The upper left pane, box 1, is the open self—all the information, behaviors, attitudes, feelings, and desires that you and others know about you, or that you would tell them about you. This is the area where you construct and preserve a coherent narrative of yourself and a stable sense of self-esteem. The upper right pane, box 2, is the blind self. This includes all the things that you don't see or know about yourself but that others recognize—from minor unconscious habits to substantial automatic defense mechanisms or approaches to conflicts. As you become aware of these things through self-observation or talk with trusted others, your communication improves.

The lower left pane of the Johari window is box 3, the hidden self. These are all the things you know, but keep secret, about yourself. When and how you disclose these things—and how much you tell—shapes the way you see others and how they see you. The lower right pane is box 4, the unknown self. This box represents nonconscious truths about you—things that neither you nor anyone else knows. The contents of this area of the self are inferred by things that appear in consciousness and take you by surprise, triggered by situational cues you hadn't noticed before.

The unknown self is the home of the early learning that shaped our basic temperament inheritance before we were five, that established our personality and became the foundation for a distinct sense of self and self-worth. Because our course focuses on effective communication for better relationships in all parts of our lives, let's discuss our earliest learning in terms of attachment theory.

Attachment theory draws on the groundbreaking work of John Bowlby and Mary Ainsworth. It states that the kinds of bonds we form as infants with our caregivers influence the kinds of relationships we form as adults. Bowlby and Ainsworth developed three types of attachment styles. Infants with a secure attachment style have caregivers who are responsive to their needs and who show positive emotions when interacting with them. These infants trust their caregivers, are not worried about being abandoned, and come to view themselves as worthy and loved.

Infants with an avoidant attachment style typically have caregivers who are aloof and distant and who rebuff the infant's attempts to establish intimacy. These infants desire to be close to their caregiver but learn to suppress this need. People who were raised with this style find it difficult to become close to other people.

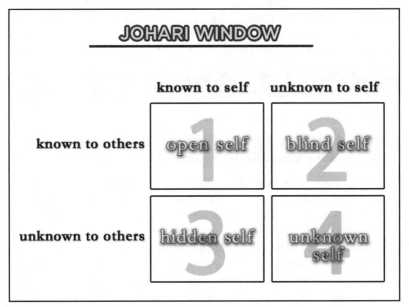

Figure 9.1

Infants with an anxious/ambivalent attachment style have caregivers who are inconsistent and overbearing in their affection. These infants are unusually anxious, because they can never predict when and how their caregivers will respond to their needs. People raised in this style desperately seek closeness to others but experience mixed, conflicted feelings even when they are in a loving relationship.

The current research and thinking is that, with conscious effort, we can modify our learned attachment style as we mature.

The current research and thinking is that, with conscious effort, we can modify our learned attachment style as we mature—by challenging the negative view of our self that it entails and by building relationships that foster secure connections in the present. This helps us rebuild our self-esteem. Let's connect attachment style directly to our definition of self-esteem: The secure attachment style clearly fosters a child's self-esteem. Parents in the other two styles, however, are treating their children as unlovable and insignificant. Whatever those children do, their behavior is criticized or ignored; they come to see themselves as incompetent. This damages their sense of self-worth and sets them up for future difficulty in dealing with other relationships. ■

Suggested Reading

Falikowski, *Mastering Human Relations.*

Exercises

1. We are sometimes awakened by an awkward communicational moment, where by accident we undermine who we think we are in a conversation (competent, involved), or someone else intentionally does that for us. Can you recall a moment when, for instance, you were caught saying something inappropriate or not paying attention? Did you notice your gaffe, or did someone else point it out to you? What did that moment feel like? What did you to do to cover yourself (notice the implication of exposure here)? Did you pretend it didn't happen and carry on; did you apologize; did you bluster and put someone else on the spot for your

embarrassment? Why would doing any of these things matter enough to do them?

2. Reflect back on how you felt your parents treated you when you were a child. Do you think the way you were raised—your attachment style—shows up in the way you relate to people in your present life? Do you think you were raised with a secure attachment style or one of the other styles?

Protecting the Self in Face-to-Face Talk
Lecture 10

The potential to undermine our sense of self and self-worth exists side-by-side with others' positive acceptance of us in every moment we talk. In fact, people have not given each other what they want—the understanding of each other's thoughts and acceptance as individuals—so many times over the millennia of human existence that as part of the cultural learning of every child, they receive a series of conscious defenses they can use to protect their self-esteem. This lecture reviews the common types of defenses and how we use them to respond to a reality that may threaten our sense of self.

L et's look at how we converse with people while avoiding situations where we risk feeling the psychic pain of embarrassment, shame, or guilt. To do that, we have to take a step back to Freud's tripartite model of the personality—id, ego, and superego. In this model, the self is powered by the id's unconscious impulses and emotions (the drive for immediate satisfaction and gratification). Society's efforts to suppress these impulses as the child is socialized are represented by the superego. This ideal self in the superego represents the larger social order inside the child's mind as well as the proper behavior required by society to limit the impulses of the id. These pressures get managed through the ego, which operates on the reality principle. The child thinks, "I really want such-and-such, but I've found in the past that when I demanded it, I got smacked, so I'm not going to ask." Thus the social order is reinforced.

What's interesting is that although Freud's version of the unconscious and its pressures on the ego is not widely accepted today, his concept of ego defenses and his list of defensive patterns are used by many therapists and researchers. When we are in trouble with reality, reality always wins—so we have to defend ourselves using one or more of these techniques:

- Denial. We simply refuse to admit that a threat is relevant to us or assume that it can be postponed somehow.

- Avoidance. We refuse to face a threat. We simply step out of the way of any situation that might force us to face weakness in ourselves.

- Rationalization. This is the most common defense. We make excuses, explaining away threats to our sense of self.

Overuse of ego defenses in our lives can mean real disconnection from reality and relationships.

- Intellectualization. This is rationalization for the better educated. They can provide more complex explanations of their own reality that will distance them from their bad behavior.

- Displacement. We redirect our reactions from a more threatening activity to a less threatening person or object.

- Projection. Rather than accept negative emotions in ourselves, we attribute our anger and threatened feelings to other people. More commonly, we simply blame others for our problems.

- Regression. With this defense, we revert to an earlier, more "childlike" state. For instance, in reaction to a stressful or unhappy situation, we say, "Let's party."

We can use our defenses to temporarily reduce anxiety by distorting our perceptions of reality (or distancing ourselves from reality). This can provide us time to overcome sudden life crises. In the short run, our defenses can help us deal with unresolvable conflicts by avoiding or denying them until we are strong enough to handle them. However, overuse of ego defenses in our lives can mean real disconnection from reality and relationships.

In his model of ego functioning and communication called transactional analysis, Eric Berne describes how we look and sound when our ego is managing reality so we don't have to deal with it directly. This model is an easy way to understand the connection between what goes on inside our bodies emotionally and how that automatically emerges in the sound of our voices, our word choices, and how we act toward others. We are always trying to get from others what we need. Berne gives three names to these internal ego states: parent, child, and adult. These names represent the general emotional states the ego can be in as it deals with the world. In turn, each of these ego states has several different levels representing a tone of voice and a style of communicating. We recognize and respond to the differing tonalities automatically. To deal with difficult talk, we need to find our adult voice—the only ego state that focuses on information and problem solving and that calls out the same state in the person we're talking to. ∎

Suggested Reading

Falikowski, *Mastering Human Relations*.

Exercises

1. The next time you are with several people in conversation, lean back and listen to the voices going by. People change their emotional positions in conversation all the time, and it shows in the way they sound.

2. As you recall a difficult conversational moment, notice the sound of your own voice when another said that you were being defensive (or notice how others sounded when you thought they were being defensive). Can you name the voice? Were you (or the other) using one of the defenses we have discussed? Which one?

3. Get conscious the next time you are confronted by someone else's criticism of your behavior or misattribution of your motives. Pause before you speak, calm yourself, and try to respond in your adult voice, describing your behavior or feelings from your point of view as if you were observing them. If the other's comments show some insight, calmly acknowledge their truth before you move on to describe yours.

Conscious Self-Talk and Self-Management
Lecture 11

Defense mechanisms and defensive talk may get us through in the short run, but in the end, they don't work. On the other hand, learning to manage our automatic, internal talk and our external responses to others does work. In this lecture, I offer you several techniques to interrupt the flow of emotional reaction and negative self-talk in difficult situations and describe a form of problem solving for difficult situations that gives you more time to respond. Momentary emotional self-management and the use of conscious self-talk radically improve our chances to be heard, understood, and accepted in tough situations. As a bonus, the repeated use of problem-solving self-talk raises our sense of self-worth and our sense of control over our lives.

Our self-talk is automatic and constant. It involves self-evaluation and almost constant evaluation of other people and the world around us. It also involves problem solving and planning for the future. Our self-talk sometimes helps us work things out, but its constancy is also a distraction from the reality around us.

Nothing less than years of meditative practice, in a distant monastery, will enable us to stop the talk in our heads, so we have to take a more practical approach to this automatic process. If we can't stop it, we can at least become more consciously aware of what we're saying to ourselves. We need to learn how to interrupt an emotional hijack; slow our internal reactions to give us time to debate with ourselves the instantaneous reality we've just created; and give ourselves a chance to recover and discover what's actually out there.

I'm going to teach you how to calm yourself with something called the centering breath. This is the type of breath that many religions use to calm the mind and move the attention to your center of energy. You need to take a breath that works in your body in just the opposite way an automatic breath does. You can try this breath sitting upright in a comfortable position, for 30 minutes, in a darkened space. Interlace your fingers and place the tips on your stomach with one of your little fingers sitting in your belly button. Close your eyes to reduce any external distractions.

Using only the nose for breathing, breathe in slowly—and as you do, push your belly out against your waistband. Your fingertips should feel the belly pushing outward as you breathe in (or upward, if you choose to practice this lying down). When the in-breath is complete, pause for just a moment, and then breathe out slowly through the nose—pulling your belly back in as you do. Continue to breathe in this manner.

In difficult moments, take a time-out and give yourself a chance to become calm.

In the centering breath, we don't move the chest or shoulders; instead we move the belly. Why? Because as we move our stomach, it opens a space for the bottom third of our lungs to expand—this is the part we rarely use in everyday breathing, the part where most of the oxygen transfer to our bloodstream occurs. In fact, if you do five of these deep breaths, you may feel a little light-headed. This is not cause for concern; it's just your brain getting more oxygen than it usually does.

In a stressful, difficult conversation, you have to interrupt the flow of emotional pressure from within and without. Try this self-management method. Step 1: Take one or two centering breaths. Step 2: Ask yourself a focusing question beginning with the words "I wonder," like "I wonder what's really going on here?" and then answer yourself internally. Say anything descriptive that you see, hear, or remember from the moment before. Step 3: Straighten your posture. This move is to trick your nonconscious brain into slowing the flow of fight-or-flight chemicals into your bloodstream. Combine this with a deep centering breath, and talk to yourself with your conscious mind. Step 4: In difficult moments, take a time-out and give yourself a chance to become calm. Politely let the other party know you need to take a quick break, and then walk away for a moment.

Here are three more questions you can use to challenge your automatic negative reactions and make your self-talk more positive and helpful: Do I have any objective data about what might have contributed to this situation?

If you know other people who've been in the same situation, did they react the same way? What advice would I give, if a friend brought this problem to me? The point of this internal debate is to shift your feelings from hot to cooler and also to shift your thoughts from absolute shoulds to preferences. All of this shifting will give you choices to deal with the reality at hand rather than denying or avoiding it so you won't feel the pain of it. ∎

Suggested Reading

Braiker, "The Power of Self-Talk."

Exercises

1. The next time you are confronted with an undermining communication, calm yourself with a deep breath and an inner dialogue of problem solving, rather than self-criticism.

2. Discover the voice of self-management and use it effectively. When you are faced with others' criticisms (unfair or not), choose not to talk to yourself from the position of the critical parent or the whiny, angry child. Instead, choose to first talk to yourself from your adult ego state. Use a calm, reasoned, problem-solving voice to argue with yourself. Practice makes better! If you do this again and again, this voice will become available to you when you have to problem solve with others in difficult situations.

Challenges to Effective Communication
Lecture 12

Communication effectiveness means that we get what we want in the situation, the other person also gets what he or she wants, and the whole thing happens in a way where we can both feel positive about the process. Calming our feelings and thinking more clearly about ourselves can help us to manage more effectively, even in difficult situations, but how does this manifest itself in our talk? In this lecture, we complete our model of self-management by outlining several ideals of thought and talk that will allow us to consciously and effectively connect with others.

Let's build an ideal model of effective thought based on two fundamentally new ways of thinking: mindfulness and appreciation. Mindfulness means waking up to what's going on within and without us in the present. We have to come to accept that we spend much of our time in a waking trance. Our cognitive unconscious, which always operates in the here and now, allows us to act without having to think about things too much in typical situations.

To be mindful, we need to do three things: First, we need to re-create categorical labels we have for the people in our memories. Second, we need to be open to new information and points of view, particularly when they challenge some of our dearly held stereotypes. Third, we need to awaken to our reliance on first impressions. When we pay attention for only a moment to what's in front of us, we leap up the inference ladder and create a "single clue" judgment.

While mindfulness is about staying focused on the present and open to new information, appreciation is about how to evaluate this new information. The values represented in the appreciative mind-set are found in three essential meanings of the word: to have a full understanding, to value and honor the other, and to add value. Think for a moment how our talk would change if we consciously committed to fully understanding a situation before we acted or spoke and valuing and honoring individuals as we spoke.

The appreciative mind-set allows us to see the useful, desirable, or positive aspects that already exist in the current situation.

The appreciative mind-set allows us to see the useful, desirable, or positive aspects that already exist in the current situation or in the people present—and to know that these can be revealed, evoked, or realized if we ask the right question. An appreciative view includes valuing and honoring the other while he or she is talking by showing respect, consideration, and direct acknowledgment of his or her value. Be sure to ask for the other's input, legitimize his or her feelings, and ask for clarification where appropriate. ∎

Suggested Reading

Kehoe, *Communication in Everyday Life.*

Exercises

1. Think of the last time that your drive to be and feel right in a complicated conversation took over your thought and speech in ways that judged another from a position of condescension or contempt because you were so certain of your position that you didn't care what the other thought at that moment. Who was the receiver of all this "rightness"—a friend, a loved one, a boss or coworker? How did it work out in the moment? Was the other persuaded and glad to have your insight, or instead resistant, threatened, or angry? How is your relationship now? Is all forgotten and forgiven, or does it seem that the other remembers your attack of "rightness" and is wary of interacting with you?

2. Write a list of six appreciations of things that happened in the recent past—things that have happened to you or that others around you have done that made you feel good. As you do this, notice your mood. Do you start feeling more positive and optimistic, even for a moment?

Talking to Connect and Build Relationships
Lecture 13

My model begins with a fundamental assumption that the first goal of all interpersonal communication is to make connections with others. In overcoming our basic uncertainty about who we are and how the world around us works, we are driven to communicate to build relationships with others and then to influence them to get what we want. The first two modes in my model of talk—connect and control talk—do just that. The third mode, dialogue talk, is about maintaining connection in the face of differences and disagreement. We are going to review the control and dialogue modes in the next few lectures, but first let's start with the mode that's at the heart of everything: connect talk.

There are two types of connect talk for building momentary but positive relationships: procedural talk and ritual recognition talk. Procedural talk is what we use to get through simple transactional situations—having a bite to eat, buying something—just to be seen as normal and performing our social roles appropriately. Where possible, we do so in a way that creates a positive emotional connection with another, even if only for a moment. We expect others (and they expect us) to enact the norms of ritual connection in a smooth and polite way because that's what "normal" people do.

The second type of connect talk involves ritual recognition or greetings, the archetypal version of which is "How are you?" answered with "Fine." We've grown up learning that this type of exchange is throw-away talk—that it doesn't mean anything—but in fact, it is the basic building block for beginning and sustaining our social connections. Like many other rituals, the words of greeting don't literally mean what they say; they have deeper meanings. The central function of both procedural and recognition connect talk is to demonstrate our ability to play social roles as a member of our community.

Once we've connected with someone, how do we continue the conversation? We use connect talk as small talk. Despite its demeaning name, small talk serves two important social functions: self-disclosure and the structuring of time. Small talk allows us a safe way to show how another can get to know us better—as we move from general topics to more personalized information, our listeners move from their first impressions of us to something more lasting.

We use procedural talk to create a positive emotional connection with others.

The first stages of sharing small talk are used to structure time in two social situations; this is called pastime talk. The first type of situation is one that requires sharing among people who are strangers brought together by a common circumstance and who are not likely to meet again: cocktail parties or long plane flights. The second type of situation is one where people who know each other meet and exchange information to deepen their positive connection. In these situations, small talk seems to be socially required, and the process of engaging in it is just as important as the content exchanged.

To summarize, ritual and small talk are safe ways for us to demonstrate our need for connection, demonstrate our ability to perform as normal speakers, and audition for new relationships. ■

Gottman, *The Relationship Cure.*

Kehoe, *Communication in Everyday Life.*

Exercises

1. Reflect on your family or an important relationship in your life. Does it feel well connected or distanced? What do you think is the positive-to-negative connect talk ratio in your relationship? Is it as high as 5:1?

2. Can you call up somebody just to say hi or call together your family just have a meal? If you haven't done that for a while, consider doing it soon. Remember, connect talk is about nothing in particular, and it's about everything.

Differences, Disagreement, and Control Talk
Lecture 14

Control talk, which is used for dealing with differences and disagreement, is divided into two types—light and heavy. This lecture focuses on light control talk, which occurs often in our daily conversation. It is the talk we use to influence or persuade others to see the world our way.

The first assumption behind problem solving with control talk is that we need to somehow manage the other or the situation to maintain or regain our face and feel right. Second, we assume that if we persist in our efforts to persuade the other, he or she will change. The third assumption is that the other person's mind works the same way our own does: We assume that our story is obvious to anyone who hears it, that it's the truth and based on real data, and that we have access to all the data we need to make this argument. The fourth assumption in our model of control talk is that the other person's resistance to our point of view is a personal matter. Our fifth assumption is that the other is to blame.

Light control talk is an automatic response to problematic interactions. This includes situations involving noticeable differences between us and the other as well as real disagreements, where differences have hardened into positions on something that's important to both of us. Light control as a form of problem-solving talk occurs in two situations: where people expect us to use it to persuade and where it emerges as our natural response to communication problems in the moment.

So let's review both of these types of situations. Light control is expected and, within certain limits of performance, accepted in key situations that recur in our daily lives. These situations have a common theme: One party to the conversation has more power than the other in that moment, and the other accepts this difference to get what he or she wants—such as expert medical advice. The forms of power used are seen as socially acceptable aspects of the role being played in the situation. Light control as persuasion works well for us when the other person has far less power than we do, has less knowledge than we do (and wants what we have), or feels he or she has little to contribute in the situation.

What about light control for solving communication problems as they emerge? When connect talk goes awry or persuasive control talk suddenly feels threatening, people are often taken by surprise and begin to have negative emotions. For example, when one person undermines the unspoken agreement about playful sharing of similarities in connect talk by saying something that is heard as critical, the other may instantly feel the need to get them to "see the light."

When we start using light control on others, they generally resist us.

What does light control talk look like in action? You start from a critical judgment about the other or the other's behavior. You then tell the other your story and his or her own story. You frame your responses with "you are" and "you should" messages to tell the other how to think, act, or feel. You listen, but only to find something you can use in your argument. To make this work, you show little or no acknowledgement of the other's side of the story. If your version of logic and rationality isn't working, then you go straight to work on the other's emotions.

When we start using light control on others, they generally resist us. They pay us back and use light control to defend themselves. Things can get very competitive, leading to frustration, rising anger, and even the worst kind of exchange—heavy control talk, which we'll discuss in the next lecture. ■

Suggested Reading

Kehoe, *Communication in Everyday Life.*

Exercises

1. Think about a time when (1) your child disobeyed an order or ignored you, (2) your spouse criticized you for reasons not obvious to you, or (3) a colleague showed up to meet you without the promised work

completed. Do you recall repeating yourself to make your point—telling the other what he or she should do or ought to have done? Perhaps you raised your voice as you repeated your critique, directly or indirectly blaming the person for your frustration by trivializing or ignoring his or her responses? How did that go for you? Did you get the person to behave differently to fit your view of the situation, or did the person actively or passively resist you?

2. In the situation discussed above, if you got your way, how did the other party seem to feel as a result? Positively motivated to change his or her ways or words? Willing to reconnect with you in the moment and continue the conversation? How did you feel about "winning"?

Commands, Accusations, and Blame
Lecture 15

The problem with light control talk is that when we use it to make others wrong, they are likely to respond by using it on us so that they can stay right. This competitive struggle can easily escalate and lead us down the path to the worst kind of talk—heavy control talk. The reason we analyze this most problematic form of talk is because it doesn't happen by accident; it is one of our built-in, natural responses to other people when they don't give us what we want. It's just the complicated and threatening end of the continuum of natural responses we have to resistance in other people.

Arguing back with others in competitive light control leads down the path to heavy control talk. Once we've undermined their arguments (and their conversational face), we hit back with "better" arguments—remembering that truth is less important than the strength of our assertion. We make arguments that are driven by plausibility rather than accuracy: arguments that sound right. Our basic assumption is that we have all the data we need; we have an answer, and we're not considering alternatives. As they continue to resist—and our feelings begin to drive our thoughts—we use more negative or hard tactics. We threaten them or call them names. Up to this point, it was just an argument about something else, but now we're beginning to feel that this is about us. They are resisting us just to make us angry or hurt us.

So how do we speak in heavy control talk? The basic speech forms of heavy control are built on the you-message. This opening phrase structures the assertion that follows so it will be taken personally. You-messages come in several forms:

- Critical labels. "You are" descriptors don't refer to the surface behavior of the person but to the person's essence.

- Commands. "Do it." When someone says this to us, it is a direct attack on our face and esteem in a conversation.

- Accusations. "You don't care," "you don't realize how I feel," or "you don't pay attention." These are the mind-reading you-messages through which we tell the other what he or she is thinking, feeling, and believing in the situation.

- Blame. "You made me." These messages are simply dishonest ways of expressing our feelings.

Once we start down the you-message path, we leave the other no choice but to react emotionally to our critical judgments, commands, or attacks.

Rationally, heavy control talk makes no sense at all. The problem that started it doesn't get solved, and the other person can't truly be made to be wrong. He or she can only be silenced. Emotionally, however, it makes tremendous sense to us. The upheaval somehow releases us from responsibility for our own bad behavior.

The worst thing about control talk in general—and heavy control talk in particular—is that no matter how the drama ends, it undermines the integrative, connective basis of the relationship. We do all of this because we don't have a natural way of talking to each other that keeps us connected even as we struggle with differences. So it's time to take action: Start learning to manage your emotions and your voice with the exercises below. ∎

Heavy control talk is a natural human response to conflict, but it never resolves the issue.

© Pixland/Thinkstock.

Kehoe, *Communication in Everyday Life.*

1. As you begin to take a conversation personally, you need to stop the conversation and calm yourself—before you say the worst thing that could come out of your mouth. Tell the other what you're about to do in your descriptive, nonjudgmental adult voice. "Actually, I need to stop for a moment here. I don't know about you, but I'm getting very upset with this talk, and I need to calm down a bit before we go on. So, I'm going to leave for a couple of minutes to ..." (get a glass of water, go to the bathroom, return to my office). Before you turn away, say "While I'm gone, I'm going to try to see this disagreement from your point of view. Just a suggestion, but maybe you could do the same for me." You're probably thinking no one ever does that; my response is right, and that's why so many of the really important decisions in our lives go badly.

2. In the situation above, once you've left the room for a moment, calm yourself with deep centering breaths. Talk to yourself in your adult voice by asking yourself a question, "I wonder why he/she doesn't want to do it my way?" Then force yourself to answer from the other's point of view rather than just sticking with your own. Keep your promise to come back to the discussion more composed, and prepared to ask them more questions and make fewer judgments. You may or may not get what you want in this situation, but even if you don't, you will have sustained the relationship, kept the lines of communication open between you and the other, and retained the ethical high ground.

Healing Relationships with Dialogue Talk
Lecture 16

Dialogue talk is the one mode of talk that is not automatic. When we are facing a communication breakdown, dialogue talk requires that we move from "reactive rightness" to a conscious choice to be mindful and appreciative in our approaches to the conversation. In making these choices, we are shifting from controlling others to managing ourselves, temporarily getting ourselves out of the way so we can think together with the other—as opposed to making up our mind first and then trying to convince the other of our view through control talk.

In dialogue talk we choose to be mindful, appreciative, meta-communicators in difficult situations—and as a result the outcomes can be far more positive than those we create using control talk. What is the nature of dialogue talk? What are its fundamental assumptions? Notice how these are really the opposite of control talk. The first assumption of dialogue talk is that I'm here to solve the problem, not to save my face. This means that I'm managing myself, not the other. The next assumption is that we both have to change. This assumption recognizes the essential interconnectedness of face-to-face talk and human relationships. In dialogue talk, we're equals. We're both involved at the same level.

In dialogue talk, I assume that my story is my story—and it's obvious only to me. Our complementary assumption is that the other has his or her story, which is obvious only to him or her. Therefore, I assume next that I will have all the data only when I listen to the other's story. Finally, in dialogue talk we always ask ourselves, how did we contribute to this situation?

Using dialogue talk requires that we make two more critical choices before we speak: (1) to manage our emotions and (2) to make a conscious choice to seek understanding of the other person before making our points in the conversation. Managing our emotions means we must take a breath, pause, and ask ourselves a question. We commit to seeking understanding first; this is a commitment to the first step in appreciation. When we learn to suspend judgment, we open the door to seeing the other's point of view. We don't do away with our own judgments and opinions—that's not really possible—but we create a space between our judgment and our overt reactions that opens a door for listening.

In dialogue talk, we have to speak so people will listen: We use descriptive I-messages. Descriptive talk means taking judgment out of our words and giving the other good information in a bad situation. This means telling the only truth we own—saying what we think, see, hear, and feel right now. Descriptive I-messages take a little practice because you-messages come to mind so easily in difficult situations.

I-message acknowledgements help us stay connected with the other, even in disagreement.

Let's practice reframing some common you-messages. "You're wrong." Instead, how about "I disagree"? Isn't that what you really want to describe—your state of disagreement? You really have no business talking about their "wrongness." Here's another one: "You aren't making any sense." Let's change this one to "I don't understand." That's all you can honestly say. The other may think he or she is making pretty good sense from his or her perspective.

I-message acknowledgements help us stay connected with the other, even in disagreement. I-message acknowledgements are inherently appreciative. They recognize the other positively even when the situation isn't working well. ■

Suggested Reading

Kehoe, *Communication in Everyday Life.*

Exercises

1. Have you ever described your feelings by telling someone else how he or she made you feel? "You make me so angry!" Doesn't that seem odd? These are your feelings; why are you talking about what you think is in

his or her mind? Descriptive I-messages are more likely to be effective because they are truthful, relevant, and clear. Practice communicating in a difficult situation in such a way that other people will still listen to you and stay connected at some level. They won't do that if you intrude into their psychological space with your judgment.

2. Can you think of the last time you openly acknowledged someone else's feelings or actions in a difficult situation? This is hard to do, because in the midst of a struggle we are usually engaged in criticizing, not acknowledging, the other. The next time that unexpected differences raise their ugly head in a conversation, try I-messages of acknowledgement instead of control talk. This is a form of meta-communication that can reduce the intensity of the negative emotions being communicated and shift the tone of the discussion away from competition to mutual problem solving.

Focus on the Other—The Heart of Dialogue
Lecture 17

> Dialogue talk is about getting the person on the other side of the problem to talk to us. In this lecture, we examine two interrelated processes: how to ask the kind of questions that will get people to talk openly; and how to listen, keep them talking, and show your understanding of what they are trying to communicate. These two processes are at the heart of dialogue talk and really matter if we want to be effective in difficult situations.

In a conversation, we already know where we stand, but we need to try and find out where the other person is. We can start by asking appreciative questions to get the information flowing. Remember, we want good information—accurate, truthful, relevant, and clear. In emotional, uneasy moments, where unexpected differences or position-taking disagreements have damaged our connection, this is the hardest information to come by.

Use open-ended questions: who, what, where, when, how, and how much. Using questions framed in an appreciative and solution-focused mode can help people clarify their own thoughts without putting them on the defensive. Instead of "Why did this happen?" try "How did this happen?" In place of "Why isn't this working?" try "What can we do to make this work?" In difficult situations, it's hard for people to hear "why" as anything but a search for blame. Then ask appropriate closed-ended questions to clarify what they've said or probe for more specific facts and details.

Listening actively is the heart of dialogue talk because it is the one act of communication that engages all of the ideals of effective talk. That's not hyperbole—if you take one thing away from this course, this is the idea to take. Active listening requires mindful attention, an appreciative mind-set, and meta-communication. It also calls for emotional self-management and a provisional, open attitude. It is called active listening because you have to be active internally and externally—making a conscious effort to do it effectively. The upside of all the effort involved is that it is the only form of talk that helps you solve problems and enhance relationships at the same time.

Listening actively requires two interconnected processes: undivided attention and understanding feedback. Make the choice to give the other your undivided attention, and then follow through. Use the body to demonstrate attention: Lean toward the speaker slightly; this communicates involvement. Face him or her with an open body position: uncrossed arms and legs. Show appropriate body movement: People feel uncomfortable talking with someone who seems highly controlled; slight movements of the head and hands to indicate encouragement are important. Also be sure to make positive eye contact. Start with the other's eyes, and move to looking at his or her face. Last, encourage the speaker to continue with your facial expression and

True listening involves hearing what others are saying from their point of view, not ours.

paraverbal and verbal encouragers ("ah," "uh-huh," "right"). The second aspect of active listening is understanding feedback. Periodically reflect back to the speaker in your own words the content and/or feeling the speaker has communicated in order to show your acceptance and understanding. Be sure to ask "Is that right?" and then listen carefully to the answer.

If the speaker is communicating his or her feelings openly, then a direct reflection will work fine. Listen for feeling words (e.g., "excited," "rejected," or "upset") and use those to guide your reflection (e.g., "You seem pretty happy about this"). Often, however, you can see that the topic evokes feelings in the speaker, but he or she does not name those feelings directly. Infer from the content and from nonverbals what the feelings could be. If the other complains about his or her personal life, you can say, "You sound pretty down about this" or "That sounds really discouraging." If you're not sure what feelings are being expressed, ask yourself what you'd be feeling in that situation. Reflecting expressed feelings back to the other can be truly connective in situations where we are separated by differences.

Keep in mind the four don'ts of effective listening:

- Don't give your opinion or advice until the other asks.

- Don't interrupt to debate the other.

- Don't tell the other what he or she should be thinking or feeling.

- Don't use the other's story as a take-off for your story. ∎

Suggested Reading

Kehoe, *Communication in Everyday Life.*

Exercises

1. Watch two people talk, ideally in complicated communication moments. Give your full attention; listen behind their words to what they are really talking about. Don't intervene and comment; just watch to discover whether they seem to be really paying attention and understanding each other.

2. Now try active listening yourself. At first, it will seem awkward (we're talkers, after all!), but the more you do it, the more natural it will become. You will also learn more about the people around you and grow closer to them.

Assertive Dialogue to Manage Disagreement
Lecture 18

When we have to deal with difficult behavior in others—actions that challenge our expectations about appropriate behavior in a particular situation—we often resort to command, a form of control talk. But command only serves to create resistance. If we want another to change, we need to assertively ask for it with dialogue talk spoken in a voice that communicates courage, calm, and clarity. In this lecture, we learn the essential steps for doing this successfully.

There are three steps to successful assertive dialogue: show up, stay in, and speak out. First let's discuss how to show up in your head in the moment. When someone does something that infringes on our sense of self or our sense of fairness, feelings of righteous indignation or anger instantly appear in our conscious mind. Our mind zooms into the past to compare this moment to other moments so we can make a judgment. But we need to stay in this moment. To do that effectively, we need to take a breath and ask ourselves "What really did happen here?" or "I wonder why they might have acted like this?"

Next, I want you to stay in the moment and prepare to speak authentically. Assertiveness starts with your adult ego state and involves self-talk focused on problem solving in the moment, beginning with three questions: "What do I want out of this situation?" "What do I think they want?" and "What can I say or do that will get me the outcome I am looking for and preserve the dignity of everyone involved?" The answers to these inner questions are communicated to the other through a firm but pleasant tone of voice, direct eye contact, appropriate facial gestures, a confident body stance, and controlled body movements.

Now we're ready to speak. Speaking out effectively in the moment means we can say what we mean and tell the other our perceptions, thoughts, and feelings about what happened. Use descriptive I-messages or you-action messages. Assertive dialogue talk shows that you have confidence in yourself and also understand other people's points of view. You respect yourself and show respect for others.

Besides the basic steps of assertive dialogue—staying present, speaking up descriptively, and asking for change—there are additional techniques that everyone can use in dealing with personal relationship struggles. One technique is to repeat as needed: When disagreements arise, people are not listening the first time they are reacting, so you have to say it again. Then, when the person comes at you with criticism, acknowledge his or her truth. When a person is behaving aggressively, he or she expects direct resistance. Try to sidestep the other's anger by agreeing with some part of what he or she says.

As you progress toward some sort of resolution of a situation, you will find additional connective statements helpful. Try a situational acknowledgement: "I know this has been tough on both of us." Or how about a blameless apology? "I'm so sorry this has happened." Finally, you can use a situational requirement description: "What else can we do? Your mother is coming on Friday." The goal is to reach an agreement to change—that works for you and the other—without beating up yourself or the other person. ∎

Telling Your Truth

Step	Goal	Action (What to Say)
Step 1	Without judgment, describe a specific behavior of the other person.	"When I see you [do this]" or "When I hear you say [that]."
Step 2	Disclose how you feel as a result, without using the expression "you make me."	"I feel ...."
Step 3	Declare the effects or impact of the person's behavior on you, your principles, values, or the situation.	"I can't focus on my work." "I lose time or money."
Step 4	Ask for the change. Describe what you want the other to start or stop doing.	"I prefer you to ..." or "I would like you to ..." or "I need you to...."

Suggested Reading

Lloyd, *Developing Positive Assertiveness*.

Exercises

1. Recall a difficult situation where you didn't get what you wanted. Write in detail the conversation as you remember it. How were you both framing your statements—in descriptive I-messages or in you-messages (or fake I-messages, such as "I think you are an idiot")? Recall the moment when you asked for change and the other refused. What had you said just before that moment? How did the refusal sound? What did you say in response?

2. Now, rework the situation above on paper using the suggested tools. See if you can invent more effective responses to substitute for what you actually said. Anticipate how the other might respond to your new approach. People almost always resist at first; so repeat as needed, and use additional connectors if you feel you might need them. Rehearse what you've written in front of a mirror until you're comfortable with the sound of your own words. You are practicing being present. If it's still appropriate, start a new conversation with that person, trying to follow your new approach.

Compassionate Confrontation
Lecture 19

This lecture reviews the steps of structured dialogue. This is a process that should be used when you've asked for a behavior change from another but haven't seen a long-term effect. The important thing to note is that this process can't be taken on lightly. It takes time, focus, patience, energy, and lots of self-management to make it work.

Structured dialogue is simply a slowed-down, opened-up form of dialogue talk: Its goal is the achievement of mutual understanding before taking action to resolve an issue. If you have a persistent problem communicating with someone, then you need to be the one to start structured dialogue. Like dialogue talk, this approach has to start in our heads. We first need to create the internal conditions that will allow us to emotionally self-manage. We can do that by committing to appreciation. Remember, appreciation means committing yourself to three elements: full understanding; valuing the other, even in disagreement; and making things better for both of you.

There are also external conditions that have to be in place for an effective structured dialogue to happen; these are fairly straightforward. First of all, choose a safe place and appropriate time. Do it when kids are not around, if you have kids. Do not attempt it just before going to bed or when either of you is already exhausted from a hard day of work. Invite the other person to the process, and make it an appointment. Set aside at least 30–60 minutes of time, because talking about persistent problems can't be done in 5 minutes.

Before you actually begin the discussion, ask the other person to commit with you to two simple process guidelines for carrying out an effective discussion: Let's not leave until the time is up, and let's try not to interrupt or attack each other. Open your structured dialogue with a statement that describes the situation from both of your points of view; I call this a mutualizing acknowledgement. Begin your sentence by saying something like "I think this affects us both ...," and then follow this up with one sentence describing your view of the problem. Use only descriptive I-messages: "The way I see it, …." But say only one sentence, and then stop!

Why would I ask you to stop? Because I don't want you to rant. The whole point of a structured dialogue is that you need to get a deeper understanding of the other's view of the situation. The best way to do that is to ask a question: "Can you tell me how you see the problem?"

The problem-solving stage occurs late in the process and is less important in many ways than the discussion itself.

Then you move on to the hard part of the process: listening actively for understanding. You have to give the other your undivided attention: Use your face, body, paraverbal, and verbal encouragers to keep the person talking, even when you're hearing things you don't like. Your appreciative commitment is to full understanding, so you have to listen for the emotional concerns behind the behavior. Be sure to provide understanding feedback periodically while you listen. If necessary, you'll have to reframe emotionally negative statements into the content that's submerged beneath the negative emotion.

Ask questions to clarify or confirm your understanding of any points the other is making. When the other seems to have put it all on the table, you can break in gently and say, "OK, do you mind if I tell my side of the story?" Seeking permission shows respect and reinforces equality, which is the basis for effective dialogue. As you're talking, ask for occasional feedback on your words; give and get clarification until you're satisfied he or she understands your side of the story.

Here's the hard news: This process is not likely to work the first time through. This is a "repeat as needed" process: Go back to step three, start the next round of the discussion with another question, get the other to talk, and listen actively. This cycle is required to reach mutual understanding. Once you have this mutual understanding, it's time to solve the problem. Negotiation and creative solution development are in order: Try some "What if we try to …" brainstorming and perhaps some creative behavior exchange to reach an agreement on an appropriate solution. Finally, agree on a decision on who will do what, when.

The problem-solving stage occurs late in the process and is less important in many ways than the discussion itself. The rule in successful problem solving is that 90 percent of the time spent should focus on developing a clear and mutually shared definition of the problem. Once that's been done, solution development and agreement can happen very quickly. ∎

Exercise

1. The appreciative approach to structured dialogue is also vital for dealing with the tensions and potential for communication breakdown that underlie any conversation we have with others from a different culture. When others do things or say things that seem odd, wrong-headed, or simply confusing, our natural reflex is to jump into criticism and control talk—which don't help the situation much. The next time you find yourself communicating with someone from a different background, use appreciative thinking and structured dialogue to slow down your judgments, create a connection, and build bridges of more complete understanding.

Communication, Gender, and Culture
Lecture 20

The one social difference that has an impact across all subcultures is gender. How we learn to view those of the opposite gender is embedded in our society's common language, and how we learn to see the world through the eyes of our gender is a critical part of our learning to see ourselves as "normal." In this lecture, we examine the differences in cultural learning that are created for children of different sexes.

How does our cultural learning affect our gender roles, and how do our gender roles, in turn, affect the way we speak? Children always learn more than just our language as they grow up; they learn our way of life, our culture, and the taken-for-granted views of the world shared by our group. Gender roles are among these learned cultural constructions. Through some instruction, but mostly by observation and imitation, we absorb the gender performance that is expected of us.

The interesting contradiction here is that while we learn to take differences in gender behavior for granted, we also learn the commonsense assumption that if everybody speaks the same language, they must be the same kind of people. So if we all speak English—using whatever accents, phrases, and words are accepted in our region—we must be using the words in the same way. But words have a variety of meanings when we're talking with folks from different subcultural backgrounds. This is the basis for considerable frustration when we talk face-to-face.

© BananaStock/Thinkstock.

Let's look at male and female patterns of talk.

Women use small talk to become closer with one another.

In her book *You Just Don't Understand*, Deborah Tannen popularized her research on the effects of gender on the style of and the intentions behind our talk. Boys grow up in a world that takes hierarchy and control for granted. There's always some boy bigger and more demanding than you in the world who's trying to push you around. As children, boys learn to use physical actions rather than words to display emotions and get what they want.

When boys mature, they use talk to do the same things. They resist responding directly to a request for service to avoid feeling in a one-down position relative to the asker. When speaking as adults, men present facts, ideas, and arguments in discussion, particularly with other men, to establish their autonomy relative to each other. They compete to get the floor in discussion, to have their say, and to maintain their independence. And in general, whether competing with other men or women, men think of talk as a tool to accomplish things—to give information, give advice, solve problems, or take a stand on an issue.

Let's compare men's report talk to what Tannen calls rapport talk for women. Unlike boys, girls develop in a world of relationships where talk is used to discover how close or distant another person is from you. Instead of larger competitive games, young girls tend to engage in smaller, more cooperative activities with other girls, so getting along is important. And unlike for men, who think of words as tools to take action, for women the rituals of speech, including feelings talk, are used to make connections before taking action.

At least to get a conversation started, women talk about personal experiences and feelings to build relationships and sustain them throughout the discussion. As a result, women take turns in speaking and generally overlap only to show support for another idea, not to take the floor away. Women are more likely than men to ask questions if they don't know something and to use speech rituals to show connection rather than competition. They also tend to use more tag questions to implicitly seek agreement and more verbal and nonverbal encouragers while listening to others.

Here are some general steps you can take to avoid the "mystery of the obvious" struggle in gender talk. Give up the assumption that we all speak the same language so the other should understand without any extra effort on your part. This means giving up the three taken-for-granted control talk assumptions: (1) I know all I need to know, so I don't have to ask. Stop mind reading and ask for information. (2) My listener must surely understand, so I don't have to reflect back what I hear or see. Don't assume the other understands you. (3) My listener feels as I do, so I don't have to notice or acknowledge the listener's feelings or give him or her a chance to express them. Acknowledging feelings is important; our feelings are what separate us from machines.

To summarize, in general men use talk to do things and to manage their independence, and women talk to build relationships and to feel connected. Both sexes need to understand these fundamental differences in their communication styles so that they don't expect the other to respond as they do. ∎

Suggested Reading

Tannen, "He Said, She Said."

———, *You Just Don't Understand.*

Wood, *Gendered Lives.*

Exercises

1. For women: Since many men think that being asked to do something comes across as an order (and they don't like to be told what to do), they often delay doing it long enough to feel that they're making their own choice to comply. So if you want the man in your life to do something, plan ahead. Make it a request for help, not a command, and leave enough time before your internal deadline so he can delay before complying.

2. For men: When your female partner asks a question about what you would like, treat this as an indirect request for herself and the opening move in a negotiation. If she says, "Would like you to stop for coffee?" don't just say "no"—be more provisional in your style. Say, "I dunno; would you like to stop?" Her next response is the "good" information you are looking for.

Talking Our Way to Lasting Relationships
Lecture 21

We are born into a web of relationships and spend most of our lives creating, sustaining, or ending them. Central to our emotional and social lives are friendship and long-term romantic relationships: Living in a caring, long-term relationship with someone we love is the key to living happier, healthier, and longer lives. Maintaining a positive connection with another unique person through the ups and downs of life requires real work and the ability to communicate effectively. Let's see how this process works.

Caring relationships meet our basic need to discover ourselves and the world around us. Without them, we can't completely fill our need to know ourselves. So how do we know if we are in a satisfying long-term relationship? Here are the three key characteristics of such relationships:

- Investment. We—and the other—give our time, energy, and mental focus to building and sustaining the relationship.

- Commitment. As a result of our continued investment in the recent past, we believe in the future of the relationship.

- Trust. Trust is built by each of us being dependable and keeping our promises.

There are also three key tensions that underlie all long-term relationships. These occur when we are trying to balance two or more desirable but contradictory actions. In openness/closedness tension, the difficulty lies in maintaining the exclusivity of our connection to the other while retaining some openness to other relationships in our lives. This tension is highest in the early stages of relationship building, when each person in the couple tries to maintain a larger social net of connections while at the same time trying to create a deeper, exclusive relationship with the other.

The autonomy/connection tension comes in because we want to maintain togetherness with our partner, but at certain points in the relationship we also may want to make our own needs or interests a priority. For instance, our need to get a better job may require moving to a new location and forcing our partner to give up a job he or she is happy with. What do we do?

Sustaining a loving relationship requires hard work but has great benefits.

The third hurdle is novelty/predictability tension. We have contradictory desires for newness and adventure on one hand and predictability and comfort on the other. After the exciting period of newness in relationship building, we create habitual patterns of behavior. The newness and discovery become balanced by predictability, but too much predictability can lead to boredom. The challenge for the couple is how to inject just enough newness into the ongoing life of the relationship to maintain interest without undermining their stable interaction patterns and pushing each other into feelings of uncertainty and fear.

The maintenance of a long-term personal relationship requires work on our part—a persistent commitment to connect talk to create a positive balance in your emotional bank account and dialogue talk for relationship repair. ■

Suggested Reading

Gottman, *The Marriage Clinic.*

Exercises

1. In your primary relationship, try to maintain the 5:1 ratio of positive to negative bid responses discussed earlier. Make polite and cheerful small talk (remember—talk about nothing means everything), and be sure to listen to your partner. The very act of giving your undivided attention reinforces your connection.

2. Do things together! Plan and carry out fun activities of all kinds, including eating at a favorite restaurant. Maintain your connective emotions by discussing past pleasurable moments and talking about your shared future.

Leadership, Appreciation, and Productivity
Lecture 22

Work is central to most of our lives, and the relationship between managers and employees is the bedrock of success for all organizations. Let's examine how the quality of this relationship can be improved by increasing the quality of the communication between them.

Like other types of cultural knowledge about how things and people work, the way our contemporary managers and employees relate is profoundly shaped by schema. The traditional Western assumptions about organizations and the roles of managers and employees were developed over a hundred years ago: An organization is a machine built of thousands of interlocking parts arranged in a hierarchy of authority. Employees are cogs in the efficient operation of this machine and are subject to control by managers above them in the hierarchy.

In this traditional model, managers were completely in charge of controlling the work, devising the best way to do it, and training workers to follow their rules. Communication was intended to serve two simple purposes in this model—to deliver orders downward and to deliver production information upward. And managers were committed to discouraging two other types of communication: bypassing (employees going around a local supervisor to talk to the manager above) and horizontal talk (employees talking with each other about how to do the work). These communication moments were considered to be either dangerous or inefficient.

We now know that to be effective, managers have to be leaders as well as controllers of the plan. They have to step outside of the traditional unconscious schema of managing and consciously invite employees to join them as partners in managing the process. Successful managers learn to lead employees so that employees can manage themselves. This not only requires managers to reenvision their role, but it also requires a conscious shift in the way they talk to their employees.

How do managerial leaders create enthusiastic or engaged employees? Managers need to see dialogue talk as a strategic tool to deal with those moments where, despite their best collaborative intentions, employees seem unwilling or unable to take on responsibility or make the decisions required of them. Recall that dialogue talk has three key elements. Managers can use description and I-messages to provide direction: "This is what the client needs." "I'd like you to start this by next Monday." Asking appreciative questions and listening actively will get employees to think about issues and solutions: "If we're going to do this better, what would you do?" Managers can use open acknowledgment and genuine support to ensure employee confidence in making and enacting decisions effectively: "You guys have done a great job in the past, and I know I can count on you again."

> **Successful managers learn to lead employees so that employees can manage themselves.**

Appreciative leaders who use dialogue talk strategically get the work done by sustaining or increasing the engagement levels of their staff. What do managers do when unexpected differences appear in their workplace? They use assertive dialogue talk and ask for change. One general rule specific to work situations is if you want people to change their behavior, it's best to have data to rely on as the basis for your request. Simply stating your opinion about change is easily resisted, and demanding change puts you back into control talk. ■

Suggested Reading

Buckingham and Coffman, *First, Break All the Rules.*

Sirota, Mischkind, and Meltzer, *The Enthusiastic Employee.*

1. If you are in a management position, practice using dialogue talk instead of control talk with your employees. For instance, say, "I noticed that you came in 20 minutes after start time this morning." Avoid using categorical labels like "late," and be specific in your description. "In fact, I checked the time sheets for the past couple of months, and you've shown up after start time every couple of weeks. Can you tell me what's going on here from your point of view?" If the other responds in a way that seems to diminish the importance of the issue, you can always describe the larger effects of his or her behavior on other individuals or on the unit as a whole.

2. For persistent problems, try using structured dialogue. Follow exactly the same steps we discussed in Lecture 19 for a couple with a persistent problem. Workplace conversations may have different content and less obvious emotional talk, but stick to the same process: Get the other person to talk first, and seek mutual understanding before going into problem solving.

Dialogue and Appreciation—Engaged Employees
Lecture 23

> To lead an effective life, we not only need to create and sustain positive relationships with friends and loved ones, but we also need to create them at work. And it turns out that the better we do that, the more productive, happy, and stress-free we are.

When we can't create or sustain positive relationships at work, we become disengaged—we lose energy, spirit, and interest. So we walk through our daily work giving a mere fraction of what we are capable of, just the minimum to get through the day. In studies, about three-quarters of people felt this kind of disengagement. When highly enthusiastic responders were asked why they were so gung-ho, and everyone else was asked what it would take to motivate them to try harder, both groups said the same thing. Let's try to learn from their feedback.

Enthusiasm came out of three elements. (1) A sense of equity—people were motivated by a sense of being treated fairly by the organization, being paid a fair wage, and not being threatened with job loss every time the organization decided to cut costs. (2) A sense of achievement—people were enthusiastic when they were able to do their best work and make a difference and when they belonged to an organization in which they could personally take pride. (3) A sense of camaraderie—employees were most enthusiastic when they could work collaboratively with others in a workplace free of threat and suspicion. Although they got pleasure from associating with others socially, their greatest satisfaction came from interacting with others on a team in pursuit of a common performance goal.

When employees don't get along with each other, or their managers, engagement falls and stress rises. Appreciative dialogue talk can help employees deal with problems more effectively and sustain their positive connection with themselves and their work. Both employees and managers need to practice replacing control talk with appreciative dialogue. They also must practice calming themselves in order to remain connected in difficult moments.

In difficult moments, the power of both the descriptive I-message and the adult voice can help clarify the issues and keep everyone engaged until a solution is found. Another workplace communication skill is cross-management. This form of dialogue talk allows employees to speak across differences in work roles or technical specialization. It keeps people connected and listening while it influences them to change.

Cross-management focuses on how to cope when firms reorganize the workplace around cross-functional teams. Most managers now accept that improving work processes requires a team of people representing different aspects of the process to be brought together to suggest improvements and reflect on how any improvements will affect them.

Employees were most enthusiastic when they could work collaboratively with others in a workplace free of threat and suspicion.

The difficulty is that even though they work for the same organization, everyone carries around stereotypical schema of other specialties or departments in their heads. It's hard to get people from different specializations to talk to each other openly and as equals—and even harder to get them to actually listen to each other.

Employees have to overcome these differences to get anything done. They overcome these differences by being reminded that the company's mission, vision, values, ideals, and bottom-line success are what brings them all together. ∎

Exercises

1. If you are in a customer service position, try these tips for using assertive dialogue talk to provide high-quality customer service and deal with difficult customers. Think a thought (e.g., "This person is upset. This is not about me. I will not take the bait."); take a deep breath; and keep a positive/neutral face. Use these tips to stay in dialogue mode: Listen actively, give the customer your undivided attention, and provide feedback to show understanding. Remember to allow the person to speak without interruption. Then acknowledge the customer's concerns (e.g., "I understand that you've been extremely inconvenienced by this delay"), give a blameless apology (e.g., "I'm very sorry this happened") and acknowledge his or her truth. Ask open-ended questions (who, what, where, when, how, and how much) to fully understand the problem, and then come up with a way to solve it.

2. Again in a customer service scenario, what should you do when the customer escalates the situation? Usually after a couple of rounds of "repeat as needed," the customer finally hears your offer of a solution. However, in a very few cases, the customer seems to think that he will somehow get more by yelling or swearing. Here is a three-tier termination process you can use to avoid further escalation. When the customer starts to lose it, begin with tier 1: "I really want to help you, but I can't do that if raise your voice (or swear at me)." Say this in your calm, well-modulated adult voice, and the customer may calm him- or herself. However, if the customer raises his or her voice again, go to tier 2: "As I said before, I want to help you, but raising your voice (or swearing at me) makes it difficult for me to help. If you continue, I'll have to call my supervisor." If he or she continues to yell, go to tier 3: "I have said twice now that I can't have you raising your voice (or swearing at me). I'm going to call my supervisor. Please wait, and I'll be right back." This is a no-surprise, dialogue talk way of asking for change, repeatedly describing the consequences if the person doesn't change, and smoothly handing off the situation when he or she won't. And if you've discussed this previously with your supervisor, he or she will know exactly what's happened when you forward the call and say, "This is a tier 3 call."

Dialogue—Ethical Choices behind Our Talk
Lecture 24

Although much talk is performed unthinkingly, we must choose to override this tendency in critical moments and make practical choices to deal positively with the difficulties we face. There are ethical implications in the practice of effective communication, not just practical ones.

We want to be effective communicators because that's how we'll get what we want out of every conversation—but we also want to maintain a good relationship with the other person. If we get what we want but leave a spouse feeling overwhelmed or an employee feeling unappreciated, then we haven't gotten what we could have gotten. Effective communication consists of getting at least some of what you wanted and also keeping the relationship intact. In the process of getting what we want, we have to manage our part of the talk so the other person also gets what he or she wants and we can both leave the moment feeling positive about the process. So the first ethical implication of effective communication is that both of us have to have gotten what we wanted.

Most of the time, our nonconscious mind is running the show—and it can get us into some very difficult communication situations. To be fully aware of the present moment, and the person in it, we have to be acting out of our fully conscious mind: engaged with the details of the moment, noticing new things, and being sensitive to changes in the context. In other words, we have to be engaged the way we were the first time we met the other—using connect talk to arouse the other's interest in us, paying close attention to the other and his or her reactions to our words and gestures, and learning about the other as he or she responds to what we say. This is another component of ethical communication: Every time you talk to someone, listen as carefully as if you were meeting him or her for the first time.

Calming our feelings and thinking more clearly about the importance of the relationship can help us to manage more effectively in difficult situations. This is more than a practical choice to solve a communication problem; it's an ethical choice about leading a better life. When we calm our minds, we can become truly mindful of the other and feel a sense of human connection. We accept the person we're talking to for who he or she is rather than wishing, wanting, or demanding that this person be different. We also reject the critical judgment with which control talk begins and sidestep our knee-jerk need to be and feel right in difficult situations.

© David Sacks/Lifesize/Thinkstock.

Appreciative dialogue talk leads to true understanding and a more harmonious world for all of us.

Accepting the present reality pulls us out of judgment and reduces the hard emotions inside of us. This allows us a chance to breathe deeply for a moment, let go of feelings of threat to our self, and discover our freedom to choose another way to look at the situation—appreciatively. When we shift to the appreciative mind-set, we are committed to fully understanding what's going on in the here and now, to valuing and honoring the other, and to improving the situation for everyone involved by using dialogue talk.

Using appreciative dialogue talk in a difficult situation positively changes the way we are in the world and the world is in us. We commit to be open, equal, and nonjudgmental in our talk so as not to impose our views on the other. We honor and value the other's existence by only talking about what we see, hear, and feel—and not about what the other ought to see, hear, and feel. We commit to staying in and with the present moment, despite the memories of the other's past words or actions or our attributions of the other's motives trying to overwhelm our consciousness. In effect, appreciative dialogue talk is more than a conversational choice: It's a life choice for nonviolence in difficult conversations. ∎

Suggested Reading

Barnlund, "Towards a Meaning-Centered Philosophy."

Stewart, *Bridges Not Walls.*

Exercises

1. Here's a variation on the well-known Reinhold Niebuhr prayer.

    Grant me the serenity

    To accept the ones

    I cannot change;

    The courage to change

    The one I can;

    And the wisdom to know

    It's me.

    The process of effective, ethical communication—and the changes it requires—starts with you. And remember, our experience always begins in failure.

2. Pick your moment to practice dialogue talk. Learn from your experience, and remember the changes you want to make the next time. Then try again.

Bibliography

Aronson, E., T. Wilson, et al. *Social Psychology.* 6th ed. Upper Saddle River, NJ: Pearson Education, 2006. This book contains two excellent chapters— chapters 3 and 4—on the low-effort (automatic) thinking we do when we see another and try to understand their reasons for acting.

Barnlund, D. "Towards a Meaning-Centered Philosophy of Communication." *Journal of Communication* 12 (1962): 197–211. This classic article adds several insights to the development of what is now the recognized model of interpersonal communication.

Braiker, H. "The Power of Self-Talk." *Psychology Today*, December 1989, 23–27. A thorough, easy-to-read overview of the relationship between self-talk, mood, self-esteem, and action.

Buckingham, M., and C. Coffman. *First, Break All the Rules: What the World's Greatest Managers Do Differently.* New York: Simon and Schuster, 1999. This is the first book to explain the fundamental forces behind employee engagement. The first three chapters lay out the research data in a truly engaging fashion.

Cohen, D., and R. Nisbett. *Culture of Honor: The Psychology of Violence in the South.* Boulder, CO: Westview Press, 1996. This research monograph outlines a series of social psychology experiments intended to confirm, at the individual level, the presence of a distinctive trait in the culture of the southern states in the United States—a predilection toward violence in response to personal insult or threat.

Devito, J. *The Interpersonal Communication Book.* 10th ed. Toronto: Addison Wesley Longman, 2004. One of the first and still a leading text for covering all aspects of interpersonal communication. It contains very good chapters introducing the basic model, intercultural influences on talk, and our choices in verbal messages.

Ekman, P. *Emotions Revealed: Recognizing Faces and Feelings to Improve Communication and Emotional Life.* New York: Henry Holt, 2004. Ekman tells the story of his research over the decades and provides accessible chapters on the nature of the central human emotions.

Falikowski, A. *Mastering Human Relations.* 4th ed. Toronto: Pearson Education, 2007. Chapters 2, 3, 4, and 8 contain clearly written overviews of established personality theories, the defense mechanisms, and transactional analysis.

Fine, C. *A Mind of Its Own: How the Brain Distorts and Deceives.* New York: W. W. Norton, 2006. An overview of important findings in social neuroscience, with humorous insights into our vain, deluded, emotional, pigheaded, and secretive brain.

Finegan, E. *Language: Its Structure and Use.* 2nd ed. New York: Harcourt Brace, 1989. Chapter 11 reviews the fundamental norms of conversation and their operation.

Gladwell, M. *Blink: The Power of Thinking without Thinking.* New York: Little, Brown, 2005. This is a well-written and interesting popular overview of what researchers are discovering about the operations of the part of our mind that we can't access with words—the cognitive unconscious.

———. *Outliers: The Story of Success.* New York: Little, Brown, 2008. In this book, Gladwell investigates another "hidden" force acting on our everyday behavior—culture and cultural learning.

Gottman, J. *The Marriage Clinic: A Scientifically Based Marital Therapy.* New York: W. W. Norton, 1999. The first three chapters provide research-based models of effective communication, dysfunction, and repair that can be applied to all long-term relationships.

———. *The Relationship Cure: A 5 Step Guide to Strengthening Your Marriage, Family, and Friendships.* New York: Crown, 2001. The first three chapters focus on what Gottman calls emotional bidding—the simple exchanges that are the essence of connect talk and the foundation of lasting relationships.

Hallinan, J. *Why We Make Mistakes: How We Look Without Seeing, Forget Things in Seconds, and Are All Pretty Sure We Are Way Above Average.* New York: Broadway Books, 2009. This book is packed with research results that describe the frailty of our rational decision-making process, including our automatic dependence on situational cues that shape our decisions.

Hofstede, G. *Culture's Consequences: International Differences in Work-Related Values.* Beverly Hills, CA: Sage, 1980. A classic piece of research still referenced in most texts published today, this work contains detailed comparisons of the values and communications styles of employees in a large international firm along 10 dimensions of meaning.

Jandt, F. *An Introduction to Intercultural Communication.* 4th ed. Thousand Oaks, CA: Sage, 2004. Chapter 10 contains excellent summaries of the work of Hofstede and subsequent researchers who expanded and adapted his original research.

Kehoe, D. *Communication in Everyday Life.* 2nd ed. Toronto: Pearson Education, 2007. This text provides a detailed look at the social and psychological forces underlying effective interpersonal communication and a detailed description of the three-mode model of talk that Professor Kehoe uses in this course.

Leathers, D. *Successful Nonverbal Communication: Principles and Applications.* 3rd ed. Boston: Allyn and Bacon, 1997. The author provides an excellent review of the research on nonverbal behavior and its effects on verbal communication, without being dry and formal.

Lloyd, S. *Developing Positive Assertiveness.* 3rd ed. Menlo Park, CA: Crisp Learning, 2002. This book outlines the tools and techniques that support the effective use of assertive dialogue.

Mehrabian, A. *Nonverbal Communication.* Chicago: Aldine Atherton, 1972. This is the research that encouraged communication theorists to focus on the impact that nonverbal behavior has on the way words are interpreted in face-to-face communication.

Pentland, D. *Honest Signals.* Cambridge, MA: MIT Press, 2008. A monograph outlining new research on our nonconscious abilities to make almost instantaneous decisions about whether or not, having just met someone, we will continue a relationship—including revelations of the behavioral bases for trust and leadership.

Plutchik, R. *The Psychology and Biology of Emotion.* New York: Harper Collins College, 1994. This research treatise outlines Plutchik's circumplex model of emotions based on measuring how the words we give to emotions connect statistically into a logical whole.

Restak, R. *The Naked Brain: How the Emerging Neurosociety Is Changing How We Live, Work, And Love.* New York: Three Rivers Press, 2006. This is an interesting overview of the research in social neuroscience, on how the cognitive unconscious part of the mind affects our relationships with others.

Sirota, D., L. A. Mischkind, and M. I. Meltzer. *The Enthusiastic Employee: How Companies Profit by Giving Workers What They Want.* Upper Saddle River, NJ: Pearson Education, 2005. Enthusiasm is at the heart of engagement. Employees are more enthusiastic—and productive—when they feel (1) treated fairly by managers, (2) a sense of achievement, and (3) a sense of camaraderie with coworkers.

Stewart, J. *Bridges Not Walls: A Book about Interpersonal Communication.* 10th ed. New York: McGraw-Hill, 2008. This collection of articles consistently enlivens our thoughts about the deepest meanings of our talk with others.

Tannen, D. "He Said, She Said." *Scientific American Mind*, May/June 2010, 55–59. On the surface, gender talk still appears different; but underneath, Tannen argues, both genders are after the same thing—hierarchy and connection in our conversations.

————. *You Just Don't Understand: Women and Men in Conversation.* New York: Ballantine Books, 1991. This is the first, and still one of the most insightful, research-based popular books written on gender and communication.

Tavris, C., and E. Aronson. *"Mistakes Were Made (but Not by Me)" Why We Justify Foolish Beliefs, Bad Decisions and Hurtful Acts.* Orlando, FL: Harcourt, 2007. This book on the psychology of cognitive dissonance explains how the process of denial of personal responsibility works at every level of political, business, and personal life.

Watzlawick, P., J. B. Bavelas, and D. D. Jackson. *Pragmatics of Human Communication: A Study of Interactional Patterns, Pathologies, and Paradoxes.* New York: W. W. Norton, 1967. A classic treatise, establishing the fundamental model of interpersonal communication we use today as well as the axioms that explain the dynamics of face-to-face talk.

Wilson, T. *Strangers to Ourselves: Discovering the Adaptive Unconscious.* Cambridge, MA: Belknap Press, 2002. This very readable treatise characterizes the nature of the cognitive unconscious side of the human mind, the research being done to clarify its operations, and what we currently know about its impact on conscious thought and talk.

Wood, J. *Gendered Lives: Communication, Gender, and Culture.* 2nd ed. Belmont, CA: Wadsworth, 2005. This is a well-written overview of the many studies done on the effects of gender on interpersonal communication.

————. *Spinning the Symbolic Web: Human Communication as Symbolic Interaction.* Norwood, NJ: Ablex, 1992. This is an excellent overview of Mead's model of the development of the self as well as the models of subsequent symbolic interactionist theorists.